# THE WOMEN'S CUSTODY SURVIVAL HANDBOOK

**Kristen D. Hofheimer, Esq.**

Word Association Publishers
www.wordassociation.com

ISBN: 978-1-59571-403-9

Word Association Publishers
205 Fifth Avenue
Tarentum, Pennsylvania 15084
www.wordassociation.com

# DEDICATION

This book is dedicated to my parents, Charles R. Hofheimer, Esquire and Diane W. Hofheimer, whose dedication to representing women in divorce and child custody cases inspired me to become a lawyer. My mother's skill at comprehending the strengths and weaknesses of a case, preparing it for trial, and advocating for mothers in custody litigation is unparalleled. My father's trial presence, understanding of the law, and ability to keep a level head and a sense of humor no matter what comes flying at him are astounding.

# FOREWORD

by Shannon Lemm, Esquire

I met Kristen Hofheimer in late 2001, towards the end of my six year child custody battle involving sexual abuse. I wish this book had been available when I was going through my case. *The Women's Custody Survival Handbook* will guide you through the landscape of court battles, custody evaluations, guardians ad litem, attorneys, and judges. It offers advice and insight into navigating unfamiliar territory which can be very frightening, especially when your children are at stake. This book is your crash course in the law and the family court system, and it is essential for any woman facing a custody or visitation challenge. This is the time to fight smart, and this book will help you do just that.

# CONTENTS

# WARNING AND DISCLAIMER

This book is based upon Virginia law. While the various jurisdictions have similar laws and processes related to child custody, the reader will find this book helpful for informational purposes. This book gives general information based upon Virginia family law and is not intended to be used as specific legal advice. Please consult with an attorney licensed in your jurisdiction with significant experience in family law for specific legal advice regarding your child custody case.

# INTRODUCTION

If you are in a custody dispute or think you may be headed there, you will find this book invaluable. Chapters 1 through 3 explain the basics: what custody really means and how it is determined, as well as when and how custody and visitation can be changed. In discussing the various custody factors, this book will give you tips about what specific kinds of information the court will be looking for, what facts can help or hurt your case, and how to present evidence in your case in support of each custody factor. Chapter 4 addresses several special issues that arise in child custody cases. If one of these special issues applies to your case, Chapter 4 will give you suggestions about how to best address your special issue and what evidence and witnesses may be key to winning your case. Chapter 5 discusses alternatives to litigation and why resolving your case outside of the courtroom, with the help of a mediator or collaborative team, may produce a better result for your family than anything a judge could rule.

Chapter 6 of this book is your courtroom survival guide. This chapter will tell you what every woman wishes her attorney would take the time to tell her in detail about court, including tips that can make or break your case. You will learn what to wear, what to expect, when to stand, and when to speak. You will learn the format of a custody trial and why you are always rushing to the courthouse and then having to wait. In addition, you will learn what to do and what not to do in order to survive cross-examination.

In Chapter 7, you will learn valuable (and money-saving) suggestions for working with your attorney. You will also learn important considerations for working with a guardian *ad litem* and other professionals involved in your case. For women who choose to represent themselves (or are forced to do so because of finances), Chapter 8 will give you the basics for acting as your own attorney. You will learn how to come to court prepared to present your evidence like an attorney and how to tell your story in an organized and persuasive manner. Chapter 9 will distill the information in this book to the short list - the 10 most important things to remember in your custody and visitation case. After reading this book, you will be empowered with insight and information about child custody so that you can walk confidently into the courtroom and present your case persuasively.

If you read this book and still need more information, visit our website at *www.virginiadivorceattorney.com* for up-to-date divorce and custody blogs, articles, and videos. You may also attend one of our upcoming live custody workshops. Please see our website for details.

# 1 WHAT IS CHILD CUSTODY?

**What does "Child Custody" mean?**

In Virginia, there are two types of custody: legal custody and physical custody. **Legal custody** has to do with having the authority to make major decisions affecting the child in question. It does not affect whether or how often a parent spends time with a child. **Physical custody** has to do with where and with whom the child resides. **Visitation** determines how and when a parent without physical custody of a child sees the child.

**Legal Custody**

Legal custody can be sole or joint. Sole custody means that the parent with sole legal custody can make the major decisions impacting the child's life without input from the other parent. When parents have joint legal custody, they are expected to discuss major decisions and try to reach consensus. Virginia courts consider decisions regarding education, non-emergency medical care, and religious upbringing to be major decisions on which joint custodians should reach agreement. Under Virginia law, there is no presumption or preference for joint legal custody or sole legal custody. It is up to the discretion of the judge who is deciding custody to determine whether to award joint or sole legal custody. Although there are a few judges who prefer to award sole legal custody, the majority of judges prefer to award joint legal custody to both parents, believing that two heads are better than one when it comes to the difficult task of raising a child. However, even these judges are faced with circumstances, such as domestic violence situations or parents who argue endlessly over everything, in which sole legal custody may be a more appropriate arrangement.

## Physical Custody

Physical custody has to do with where and with whom a child resides. Physical custody can be **primary physical custody** (sometimes called **sole physical custody**), **shared physical custody** (sometimes called **joint physical custody**), or **split physical custody**. Additionally, some people prefer to use the term "**parenting plan**," rather than custody, to describe the physical custodial arrangement.

Primary physical custody means that the child lives primarily with one parent and has visitation with the other parent. Shared physical custody means an arrangement by which both parents spend significant amounts of time with the child. The parents may have equal time with the child, but not necessarily. Shared custody may refer to many different sorts of arrangements under which each parent has the child for a good portion of the time.

Under the child support guidelines, shared custody refers to a situation in which the parent without primary physical custody spends over ninety days per year with the child. In determining how many days the visiting parent has, the Virginia code has specific definitions for what counts. A day is defined as a 24 hour period of time. So a weekend from 6:00pm on Friday until 6:00pm on Sunday would count as two days. If the parent has an overnight visit of less than 24 hours, it counts as half a day. For example, if the parent picks up the child from school on a Wednesday, keeps him overnight, and returns him on Thursday morning, that period of time counts as half a day for shared custody child support purposes. Any visit that does not include overnight visitation does not count at all for purposes of determining the number of days per year of visitation. It is important to note that the ninety day re-

12

quirement and the definition of a day are only important in determining child support. There is no ninety day requirement for determining whether a custody arrangement is or is not called shared custody for purposes of determining custody and visitation.

Split custody refers to a scenario in which parents have more than one child together, and the custodial arrangement is not the same for each child. For instance, if the parents had two children and the mother had primary physical custody of one of the children and the father had primary physical custody of the other child, it would be considered split custody. Courts typically do not like to split up siblings. Often when parents have a split custody arrangement, it is because the parents determined for themselves that split custody was best for their family rather than because a judge ordered it. However, there are situations when a court will order split custody. For example, when an older and mature teenage child has a strong preference to live with a parent other than the one that the court determines is best for the younger children, then a court will order split custody.

**Visitation**

Visitation (sometimes referred to as **parenting time**) refers to the time that the parent without physical custody spends with the child. Typically, visitation includes overnight and extended periods of time spent with the non-custodial parent in his or her home or the place of his or her choosing, but in special circumstances, visitation can be supervised or can take place in a therapeutic setting.

# 2 HOW DO COURTS DECIDE CHILD CUSTODY AND VISITATION?

In Virginia, as in most states, child custody and visitation determinations are made based upon the idea of the "best interests of the child." The court looks at specific factors with respect to the parents and the child in question. After analyzing the factors, the court's task is to make a custody and visitation determination which serves the best interests of the child. In Virginia, these factors are as follows:

**Child Custody and Visitation Factors**

1.  The age and physical and mental condition of the child, giving due consideration to the child's changing developmental needs;
2.  The age and physical and mental condition of each parent;
3.  The relationship existing between each parent and each child, giving due consideration to the positive involvement with the child's life, the ability to accurately assess and meet the emotional, intellectual and physical needs of the child;
4.  The needs of the child, giving due consideration to other important relationships of the child, including but not limited to siblings, peers and extended family members;
5.  The role that each parent has played and will play in the future, in the upbringing and care of the child;
6.  The propensity of each parent to actively support the child's contact and relationship with the other parent, including

whether a parent has unreasonably denied access to or visitation with the child;

7. The relative willingness and demonstrated ability of each parent to maintain a close and continuing relationship with the child, and the ability of each parent to cooperate in and resolve disputes regarding matters affecting the child;

8. The reasonable preference of the child, if the court deems the child to be of reasonable intelligence, understanding, age and experience to express such a preference;

9. Any history of family abuse. Family abuse is defined as any act involving violence, force, or threat including, but not limited to, any forceful detention, which results in bodily injury or places one in reasonable apprehension of bodily injury and which is committed by a person against such person's family or household member. If the court finds such a history, the court may disregard [factor #6].

10. Such other factors as the court deems necessary and proper to the determination.

In this chapter, I will discuss each of these factors in detail, including what evidence the court will be interested in when analyzing each factor.

**Factor #1: The age and physical and mental condition of the child, giving due consideration to the child's changing developmental needs.**

In analyzing this factor, the court is interested in the child herself. How old is she? Does she have any health issues that the court should be considering? What about any emotional or intellectual special needs? What are the child's specific developmental needs at this time, and what developmental needs will be arising in the foreseeable future? You will need to be prepared to address these questions in an organized manner by presenting **admissible evidence**. As much as you would like to put all of your information in front of the judge, courts are only permitted to view, hear, and consider evidence which is considered admissible under the rules of evidence. I will briefly discuss basics of evidence in this book, including the rule that you will probably have to deal with the most, the **hearsay** rule. Please refer to the **What is Hearsay?** section of this book for more on the hearsay rule.

If your child is healthy and has no special needs, this factor will be easy to address. You may just need to brush up on some of your child rearing reference books in order to articulate what you believe to be your child's current and foreseeable developmental needs (such as attachment, intellectual stimulation, socialization with peers). If you have a child with special needs, you will need to be able to present your child's special needs to the court, and you will likely need to use an expert witness to testify about your child's special needs and how those needs are best met. If your child is an infant or a toddler, breastfeeding and attachment are issues that may need to be addressed here. I will discuss the issue of **custody and visitation with a breastfeeding child** in the **Special Issues in Child Custody** section of this book. Attachment and separation anxiety are issues that may need to be addressed by an attachment expert. If your child is school-age, you may wish to present evidence regarding which custody and visitation arrangement will best promote your child's  academic and social success in school. With a teenager, you may choose to present evidence about your child's wishes (see more under factor #8), or about how a proposed custody arrangement will impact his significant extracurricular activities. Factor #1 is about your child, who she is, and what she needs.

**Factor #2: The age and physical and mental condition of each parent.**

The court must consider the age and physical and mental condition of each parent. Generally, the age and physical condition of the parents are not major issues. So long as each parent is capable of providing care for the child, the court is not going to award custody to the parent who is younger or more physically fit. The mental condition of the parents is another story.

The Virginia courts and legislature have gone around and around in the last several years on the issue of whether a parent's therapy records, and/or testimony by a therapist regarding a parent, can be obtained or is admissible as evidence in a child custody case. As of July 1, 2008, the statute which kept these records confidential and inadmissible in custody cases was repealed, and the records and/or testimony may be admissible due to the fact that the mental condition of the parents is a factor that the courts are required to consider.

Often, if the mental health of a parent is at issue, the court will order a psychological evaluation of one or both parents. Additionally, expert witnesses can provide testimony about mental health issues. Be forewarned that although you can give testimony about behaviors that you have witnessed on the part of your child's father, you cannot diagnose him as being mentally ill. Only a qualified mental health evaluator or provider can do that. Attempts on your own to portray or describe your child's father as "crazy" may end up backfiring against you and making you look vindictive. If you are concerned about the mental health of your child's father, you may want to consider requesting a psychological evaluation of him, but only after careful consultation with your attorney. If you request a psychological evalutation of him, he will probably request one of you. Psychological testing is not foolproof. Your spouse may come out with flying colors, even if he is not psychologically sound. On the other hand, you may come out as having some traits of concern simply by virtue of the stress and fear that the custody litigation is causing you. A biased evaluator or skewed test data can cause irreparable damage to your custody case.

**Factor #3: The relationship existing between each parent and each child, giving due consideration to the positive involvement with the child's life, the ability to accurately assess and meet the emotional, intellectual and physical needs of the child.**

This factor addresses the quality of the relationship between each child and each parent. While courts are usually reluctant to make a custody determination which separates siblings from one another, it is not uncommon for children in a family to differ in the quality of their relationships with each respective parent. The quality of one child's relationship with a parent may impact a custody determination for all of the children in a family, if the relationship is profoundly positive or negative. If there is an unusually strong bond between a parent and one or more children, it is important that the court sees that the relationship is an appropriate parent/child relationship, not a peer-type friendship and not one in which the child is providing comfort and support to the parent. You must be extremely careful, especially if your relationship with the other parent ended due to his infidelity or you are simply devastated by the breakup, that you are not putting your child in the role of confidant and emotional nurturer. Additionally, mothers are particularly susceptible to being accused of being "enmeshed" with their children. Therefore, while you want to portray for the court the positive and unique qualities of your relationships with each of your children, you must take care to demonstrate that you observe appropriate parent/child boundaries in those relationships.

When courts do allow children to testify or to speak to the judge in chambers, the court is more likely to ask them about their relationship with each parent, rather than asking them directly which parent should have custody. In these situations, the court is usually more interested in hearing from the child about her relationship with each parent and how each parent is able to assess and meet the child's various needs, than with which parent the child wants to live with. The court is tasked with making a decision based upon what the court determines to be in the best interest of the child, not necessarily on what the child wants. This is a factor for which a child may be able to give the court significant insight.

In order to demonstrate to the court that you are able to accurately assess and meet the child's emotional, intellectual and physical needs, you should be able to articulate to the court what you

18

think those needs are, and how, as custodian of the child, you plan to meet those needs. You may also wish to call witnesses, such as teachers, counselors, and health care providers to testify about their assessment of what the child's needs are and their observations of your ability to accurately assess and meet those needs. If you have a special needs child, this factor may be of particular significance in this case. The court will be interested in how well-equipped you are to deal with your child's particular needs and challenges.

**Factor #4: The needs of the child, giving due consideration to other important relationships of the child, including but not limited to siblings, peers and extended family members;**

This factor focuses on the child's needs, particularly with respect to continuing the child's important relationships. You will want to provide evidence that shows that, in your custody, the child will be able to maintain his relationships with neighborhood and school friends, siblings (including step and half siblings), grandparents, aunts, uncles, cousins, and anyone else who has played an important role in your child's life. You may want to have a neighbor testify about her child's relationship with your child, or make a map of the neighborhood showing the proximity of all of the children that your child plays with. You may wish to have your parents or siblings testify about your extended family activities and traditions and their unique relationships with your child.

**Factor #5: The role that each parent has played and will play in the future, in the upbringing and care of the child.**

This is the factor under which the parent who has been the primary caretaker of the children should get some credit. Often, women mistakenly think that the court will award them custody without much of a challenge because they have been the ones to care for their children, from prenatal care to hourly infant feedings to diaper changing to pediatrician visits to being there when the school bus comes to providing a snack and homework help or being the one to miss work when a child is home with the flu; while the children's father had minimal involvement in the day-to-day aspects of child-rearing. Wrong!!! This is but one of the ten factors that courts consider when awarding child custody. However, this is the factor in which, for most families, women prevail. Make the most of it! You will likely have a whole lot of information about your role as the children's primary caretaker. You could probably go on for hours, if not days, about the things that you have done for your child from the day she was born, things which no one else in the universe, including your child's father, had any interest in doing. However, you can also count on the fact that the court is not going to give you days, or probably even hours, to give this testimony. Because of this, it is very important to organize your information in such a way that you can present it in court in an abbreviated manner without discounting its importance.

If you are working with an attorney, you should write a narrative for your attorney, outlining all of the things that you have done and continue to do for your child. You should also make sure to let your attorney know the things that your child's father has done and continues to do, so that your attorney will not be caught by surprise in court. If you have a **guardian *ad litem*** or **custody evaluator**, you may also wish to provide this narrative to them. However, if you are providing documentation to a guardian *ad litem* or custody evaluator, you should self-edit more than you need to with your own attorney; be straight-forward, factual, and brief rather than providing a rambling narrative. Focus on your strengths, rather than your child's father's weaknesses, and, above all, do not provide the guardian *ad litem* or custody evaluator with a lengthy, written diatribe about the faults and shortcomings of your child's father. To do so will probably make you, rather than the other parent, look bad in the eyes of these people who have a significant voice in your case.

Whether or not you are working with an attorney, you should be able to summarize in your testimony who takes care of the basics in child rearing:

1. Who gets the children up, fed, and off to school/daycare in the morning?
2. Who makes the doctor/dentist/therapy appointments and takes the children to the appointments?
3. Who stays home when a child is sick?
4. Who finds and registers for summer camps, sports, and lessons?
5. Who helps with homework?
6. Who feeds the children dinner?
7. Who bathes them?
8. Who puts them to bed?
9. Who goes to parent/teacher conferences?
10. Who makes sure the children have clean clothes that fit when they have to be dressed for an occasion?
11. Who plans birthday parties and holiday activities for the children?
12. Who arranges play dates?

This is a factor for which you will probably be your most important witness. You may choose to call lay witnesses, such as teachers, neighbors, and friends to corroborate your testimony about your involvement with your children. Other corroborating evidence can include school records (who signed the report cards and homework log?), calendars, medical records (who brought in the children?), and daycare records (who signed the children in and out?), although you will need to work within the rules of evidence to get these records admitted into evidence in court. Another method of organizing this information in a way that makes it easy for the court to comprehend is to make a chart of the child care activities and what percentage of responsibility each parent has for each activity. If you and your child's father have been living separately for some period of time, it may also be helpful to make a pie chart of the time the child has spent living with the two of you together and living with each parent separately.

**Factor #6: The propensity of each parent to actively support the child's contact and relationship with the other parent, including whether a parent has unreasonably denied access to or visitation with the child.**

This is one of Virginia's two "friendly parent" factors. Many jurisdictions require courts to consider which parent is more likely to cooperate with the other parent and promote the relationship between the child and the other parent. Many judges will say that they consider the friendly parent factors to be the most important in making custody/visitation decisions. Mothers often get tripped up on the friendly parent provisions. This is frequently due to the fact that during the marriage or relationship with the child's father, most or all of the child-rearing responsibilities were delegated to the mother. She handled healthcare, dental care, and therapy issues for the children on her own. She went to school functions, PTA meetings, and parent-teacher conferences on her own. She scheduled play dates and recreational activities on her own. During the marriage or relationship, it never occurred to anyone that the fact that she did these things on her own meant that she was trying to deprive the father of his relationship with his child. She was simply fulfilling her responsibilities within the family unit. Chances are, if this was the family division of labor, the father never asked about doctor and dentist appointments or PTA meetings. These were chores. Post-separation, it makes sense that the mother would not change the way in which she took care of child-rearing tasks. However, this same approach to child-rearing responsibilities, post-separation, could result in an accusation that the mother is trying to alienate the child from the father and make her appear to be an "unfriendly parent."

Additionally, in highly contested cases, the father will set a "friendly parent trap." Remember, the court must consider whether a parent has unreasonably denied access to or visitation with the child. In order to make you look as if you do not support his contact with the child or have unreasonably denied him access, he will start making requests for contact like never before. If you have custody, he may suddenly begin asking for an extra night each week, or to bring the child home at an unreasonable hour on a school night. If he currently has custody, he will create a situation which makes it extremely inconvenient for you to exercise your visit. If you acquiesce, the requests will keep coming, like the mouse who first only wanted a cookie and then needed a glass of milk, etc., until you finally have to say no. If, on the other hand, you react negatively, he will use that reaction as proof that you do not support his contact with the child.

If your child's father begins putting you on the spot with requests, you should take some time to think out and/or discuss with your attorney how you should respond. It is fine to say to him that you need some time to look at your calendar and think about whether the idea is best for your child. Discuss the request with your attorney and decide whether it is best to give in and show how unremittingly reasonable you are, or whether you should take a deep breath and counter with a calm, "No, I do not think it would be best for Junior to attend the Wet Tee-Shirt Competition with you this Wednesday night, but he would probably enjoy going to the Children's Museum with you right after school on Wednesday." It is always a good idea, when turning down an unreasonable request, to give a reasonable counter-offer. If you can do it in writing (e-mail is always easy), then you will have a record of your efforts to allow him reasonable time with the child if he ever accuses you of failing to support his contact with the child.

Even if your child's father had no interest in your child's school, health care, and extracurricular activities while you were together, once you enter the world of child custody litigation, you can expect that he will suddenly become fiercely interested. It is to your benefit, no matter how cumbersome it sounds, to share information about these things with him, and to do so in a timely manner. If you take the time to do this, and he still remains uninvolved, so be it. That fact will help you in your custody case. If he suddenly starts showing up at every teeth cleaning appointment and camp physical wearing his "World's Greatest Dad" tee-shirt, try not to lose your composure. He now has an attorney instructing him how to be a parent (funny how he listens to his attorney's advice on how to raise your child more than he ever listened to yours...). Resist the temptation to say something sarcastic. If you do, you will undoubtedly hear the same words repeated in court. And the judge's sense of humor is probably not as keen as yours. Try to take yourself out of the equation and focus on how glad your child must be to suddenly have dad observing his every flouride treatment and height and weight measurement.

If you are under a court order to provide specific visitation, consult with an attorney before you ever withhold a court-ordered visit, even if you believe that you have very good reason to do so (see chapter 4 on abuse), as to do so can have dire consequences for your custody case. If there is an issue that you think justifies withholding visitation, try to set an emergency hearing on the issue before the next scheduled visit.

Because the friendly parent provisions tend to work against the parent who has had the most responsibility for the child, it is very important that women be wary of friendly parent traps and make efforts, within reason, to support and promote the father/child relationship. It is also important to be able to counter claims that you have not promoted the relationship by documenting your efforts via e-mail or by keeping them contemporaneously on a calendar.

**Factor #7: The relative willingness and demonstrated ability of each parent to maintain a close and continuing relationship with the child, and the ability of each parent to cooperate in and resolve disputes regarding matters affecting the child.**

This is the other friendly parent factor. It is sort of a disjointed one because the first part is concerned with whether each parent has maintained a relationship with the child, which does not seem to have a lot to do with each parent's ability to cooperate in and resolve disputes regarding the child. For the first part, which is somewhat diluted by the second, you simply need to present evidence that you have continued to keep a close relationship with the child and are willing to continue to do so. If the father has been an absentee parent, whether you and he were together or not, you would want to present that evidence, as well.

Again, judges seem to place particular emphasis on the friendly parent provisions. Generally, judges have little tolerance for parents who are unable to reach compromises between themselves in the rearing of their child. While this makes sense, there are situations in which it is unrealistic and unfair to expect a parent to be able to resolve disputes with the other parent without outside intervention. In cases of domestic violence, or where a parent is controlling or narcissistic, there is no level playing field in which real cooperation and dispute resolution can take place. What does take place is bullying and succumbing to a bully, which serves only the bully's interests and not the child's.

If there is a level playing field, by all means, cooperate and resolve disputes wherever possible. Keep a journal, log, or calendar in which you can document your efforts to cooperate. Keep e-mail communications which shows your efforts to compromise and resolve disputes. These can be important pieces of evidence for this factor. If there is not a level playing field, and you are not able to work together to resolve disputes, you will need to be able to justify this. Please see my comments under Factor #9 if there is a history of domestic violence. If you are dealing with narcissistic or controlling behavior, you will need to put on evidence to show the judge this behavior and why it inhibits you from being able to resolve disputes.

Often, if you are trying to parent with a controller or narcissist, you will be able to find e-mails or other communications in which your child's father shows his true colors. These e-mails, in his own words, are worth a thousand of your words in trying to explain his behavior to the court. Keep any abusive, controlling, or berating e-mails that he sends to you. They are invaluable for use in cross-examining an abusive, controlling, or narcissistic parent who claims that you do not cooperate with him in resolving disputes.

**Factor #8: The reasonable preference of the child, if the court deems the child to be of reasonable intelligence, understanding, age and experience to express such a preference.**

I am often asked how old a child has to be in order to be able to choose which parent he wants to live with. The simple answer is 18. As long as a child is a minor, it is up to the court (if the parents cannot agree), not the child, to determine the child's best interest and make a custody decision accordingly. With that being said, judges vary on the issue of whether and under what circumstances they will allow children to give their input, and on how much weight to give that input.

If the child has a guardian *ad litem*, who is an attorney appointed to represent the best interests of the child (please see the section on guardians *ad litem* in Part V), your judge may not want to hear from the child. The judge may only want to hear what the guardian *ad litem* has to say. The guardian *ad litem* is supposed to let the court know the child's wishes even if those wishes are contrary to what the guardian *ad litem* recommends.

The court is supposed to allow your child to testify in open court, if you choose to call her as a witness. If both parents agree, the judge may speak to the child in chambers without the parents or their attorneys present. In that case, the guardian *ad litem* will probably be present, as well as a court reporter to take down what is said in chambers. While this is the protocol which is supposed to be followed, some judges do it differently. The court is supposed to make a determination that the child is of reasonable intelligence, understanding, age and experience to give the court input. Often, courts decide that around the age of 12, it is appropriate to speak to children. Typically, the older a child is, the more weight the court

26

will give to her preference. Most courts will acknowledge that once a child is old enough to drive, it does not make much sense to order her to live in a home where she clearly does not want to be, absent extraordinary circumstances.

**Factor #9: Any history of family abuse. Family Abuse is defined as any act involving violence, force, or threat including, but not limited to, any forceful detention, which results in bodily injury or places one in reasonable apprehension of bodily injury and which is committed by a person against such person's family or household member. If the court finds such a history, the court may disregard [Factor #6].**

The court is supposed to consider whether there is a history of family abuse in making child custody and visitation determinations. If you are able to prove, to the court's satisfaction, that there is a history of abuse, then the court may disregard the factor which requires you to promote the relationship between the child and the other parent, with the idea being that it is not reasonable to require a parent to support an abusive relationship. I discuss the issue of custody and visitation determinations in cases where there has been abuse in the chapter in this book devoted to that issue. You should be aware that when you raise the issue of family abuse, the abuser is likely to not only deny that he is abusive, but also to claim that you are making a "false allegation" of abuse with the intent of depriving him of a relationship with his child. As I will further explain in the chapter on abuse, it is extremely important to proceed with caution when raising the issue of abuse. If possible, you should work with an attorney who has significant experience in dealing with issues of abuse in child custody cases, and you should also make sure that you have sufficient admissible evidence of the abuse so that you can counter any claim that you are making a false abuse allegation.

**Factor #10: Such other factors as the court deems necessary and proper to the determination.**

This factor is the catch-all for other issues which may be important to the court in determining child custody. Under this factor, the court may consider any special facts or circumstances in your case that the court deems relevant to making a custody and visitation determination regarding your child. Some such circumstances will be discussed in depth in the **Special Issues in Child Custody** part of this book.

Once the court has heard evidence and argument, it will make a child custody and visitation determination based upon the ten custody factors. The court must consider the factors, but does not need to specifically state what weight was given to each factor. Because of the number and breadth of the factors, the court has a great deal of discretion in making child custody determinations.

# 3 CHILD CUSTODY ORDERS AND MODIFICATION

Courts have continuing jurisdiction to modify court orders pertaining to children. In Virginia, an initial determination of child custody can be made in the juvenile and domestic relations district court (which I will refer to as the juvenile court, but which is also sometimes referred to as the J&D court or JDR), or in the circuit court if child custody and visitation are being determined as part of a divorce proceeding. In either court, the judge can make a temporary, or *pendente lite*, child custody and visitation order while the trial is pending. Legally, this temporary custody determination is to create a stable situation for the child while the custody case is pending, but has no effect on the outcome of the pending case. In reality, custody cases can drag on for months or even years, and the temporary order, to which the child becomes accustomed, can set a precedent which may be difficult to undo in the custody case. Typically, at the onset of a child custody and visitation case, the court will issue a temporary order, appoint a guardian *ad litem* for the child, require both parents to attempt mediation, require both parents to attend a class on co-parenting, and set a trial date. After trial, the court will enter a final custody and visitation order.

If your case is decided in the juvenile court, you have an automatic right to appeal to the circuit court, as long as you follow the procedure for noting an appeal within 10 days of entry of the order that you are appealing. The appeal to the circuit court is known as a *de novo appeal,* which essentially means that it is a "do over," and the case is treated as if the trial in the juvenile court never happened (although unless you are granted a stay of the juvenile court's order, you have to follow that order until a new order is entered in the circuit court). Once you have a final order in the circuit court, whether as a result of an appeal from the juvenile court to the circuit court or as a result of a custody determination made in a divorce case, you may file an appeal to the Virginia Court of Appeals within 30 days of entry of the circuit court order. The court of appeals will not consider any new evidence, but will look at the record from the trial in the lower court and read briefs and legal argument to determine whether the lower court erred in its application of the law or abused its discretion in making findings. Because trial judges have such broad discretion in making child custody and visitation determinations, it is rare for the court of appeals to reverse a finding of the trial court. In the event you wish to further appeal to the Virginia Supreme Court, you may ask the Virginia Supreme Court to hear your appeal. However, unless the issue that is the basis for your appeal is one that the court wishes to consider and make a ruling on, the court is unlikely to consider an appeal at the supreme court level in a child custody case.

Once you have your final custody and visitation order, either party may file for a modification of custody and/or visitation. In order to modify custody or visitation orders, the person wishing to modify the order must first prove that there has been a material change in circumstances since the time the last final order was entered, and then prove that the requested change in custody or visitation is in the child's best interest, using the child custody factors discussed in Chapter 2.

# 4 SPECIAL ISSUES IN CHILD CUSTODY

Often, there are special issues in child custody cases which must be addressed. They may require the use of **expert witnesses**, who are people who have expertise in a particular area of knowledge, through education and/or training, who can help to educate the court about an issue and provide an expert opinion. If you have a special issue in your case, it is very important that you address the issue thoroughly and educate the court about your issue so that it is not disregarded and so that the court does not make an uninformed decision regarding the issue. Additionally, when you do have special issues in your custody or visitation dispute, you should consider collaboration or mediation, which may allow you to more closely address the unique needs of your child and your family than the more "cookie cutter" approach to custody and visitation that the court may take. In this chapter, I will discuss some of the special issues which arise in child custody and visitation cases.

### Breastfeeding

Do not make the mistake of assuming that a court will make custody and visitation rulings around the fact that a child is nursing. Courts generally do not place primacy on the breastfeeding relationship. Often, judges will believe that breastfeeding does not need to be an issue, since formula is available and plenty of parents bottle-feed. Or, judges may support breastfeeding but think that mothers can simply pump and store breastmilk indefinitely, and so the fact that the child is breastfeeding need not be considered. Additionally, courts may decide that a certain age is long enough, and after that age, breast-feeding should stop. Some courts may even determine that breast-feeding after a certain age shows that the mother is overly "enmeshed" with the child or is using breastfeeding as a way to undermine the child's bond with the father.

If you are involved in custody and visitation litigation with a nursing infant or child, you will need to educate the court about a) the benefits of breastfeeding; b) the mechanics of breastfeeding (why you cannot simply pump a week's worth of breast milk and send your child off for a week); c) the role of breastfeeding in the child's forming attachments with both parents; and d) weaning (how and when it may occur, the possible repercussions of abrupt weaning to satisfy a court-ordered custody/visitation order). Ideally, you would have several expert witnesses to address each of these components of breastfeeding:

A pediatrician can address the physiological benefits of breast-feeding. The pediatrician may also be able to discuss the American Academy of Pediatrics Policy Statement on Breastfeeding and the Use of Human Milk, which is very supportive of extended, on-demand nursing.

A lactation consultant can address the mechanics of breast-feeding, such as how let-down occurs, the need for continuous physical contact between an infant and a mother in establishing breastfeeding, how long it is reasonable to expect that the child and mother can be separated and still maintain breastfeeding, the limitations of pumping breast milk; and can address, to some extent, what can happen if the child is weaned too abruptly. The lactation consultant will probably be the least costly of the expert witnesses that you will use, but may well be the most important. The court is probably less familiar with the mechanical realities of nursing a child than the fact that breastfeeding is beneficial.

An attachment expert can address the role of breastfeeding in the child's formation of secure attachments, not only to his mother, but also to his father and to others. The attachment expert can also address the developmental benefits of breastfeeding beyond the

32

time when the immunilogical and nutritional benefits become less important, and the possible repercussions of abrupt weaning. Finally, the attachment expert can discuss appropriate custody and visitation schedules for very young children, whether or not the court supports breastfeeding.

While using expert witnesses can become quite expensive, they may be necessary if you are in litigation and the court needs to be educated on important issues. For a very detailed discussion on the issue of breastfeeding in custody/visitation cases, see Kristen D. Hofheimer, *Breastfeeding as a Factor in Child Custody and Visitation Decisions*, 5 VA. J. SOC. POL'Y & L.433 (1998).

## Same Sex Relationships

The issue of same sex relationships in custody and visitation determinations is currently in a period of flux throughout the United States, even in Virginia, which is one of the most actively anti-gay areas in the country. While Virginia has held that homosexual conduct does not *per se* render a parent unfit, the most recent Virginia Supreme Court substantive decision on child custody, when the proposed custodian is in an active same-sex relationship, held that the lesbian mother should not have custody because conduct inherent in a same-sex relationship (sodomy) was illegal, and therefore the mother was engaged in illegal activity, and that the child may suffer from social condemnation as a result of living in a lesbian household. *See Bottoms v. Bottoms*, 249 Va. 410; 457 S.E.2d 102 (1995).

There has been a recent ruling by the Virginia Supreme Court involving a custody dispute between a biological mother and her former same-sex partner which may, at first blush, appear to support recognition of the same-sex relationship, but the decision was based upon procedural rules and not upon the substance of the case. *See Miller-Jenkins v. Miller Jenkins*, No. 070933 (Va. June 6, 2008).

The substantive issue of child custody with a parent engaged in a same-sex relationship has not been addressed by the Virginia Supreme Court since the United States Supreme Court found laws prohibiting sodomy between consenting adults to be unconstitutional in 2003. *See Lawrence v. Texas*, 539 U.S. 558 (2003). Although Virginia still has not repealed its sodomy statute, the U.S. Supreme Court has stricken laws against consensual sodomy between adults. Thus, one of the bases for denying the lesbian mother custody in the Bottoms case, that she was engaging in illegal activity by engaging in sodomy with her partner, no longer applies. The other rationale in the Bottoms case, the potential for social condemnation, is also in flux. For one, that basis for denying a mother custody has potential for constitutional challenge. The same rationale was formerly used to deny custody on the basis of race, and was found to be unconstitutional in that context. *See Palmore v. Sidoti*, 466 U.S. 429 (1984). Furthermore, even in Virginia, homosexual households are becoming more visible, and societal attitudes are changing, rendering the idea that a child raised in a homosexual household may suffer from social condemnation more and more speculative.

In an unpublished 2007 case in the Virginia Court of Appeals, a father engaged in a homosexual relationship attempted to raise these issues. However, because they had not been raised in the custody trial itself, the Court of Appeals was not able to consider them. *See AOV v. JRV*, Nos. 0219-06-4; 0220-06-4 (*unpublished*) (Va. App. February 27, 2007). These issues are ripe for consideration now.

While the Virginia Supreme Court's stance in the Bottoms case is currently Virginia's official position on the current status of the law, I have found in my cases involving lesbian and gay parents that most trial judges are far more interested in which household is more focused on the needs of the child and which parent better promotes the child's relationship with the other parent, than on the sexual orientation of the parents. I have yet to find a judge who would rule out a parent as a custodian based solely on that parent's sexual orientation. I practice throughout the Commonwealth, and have found this to be true even in the more conservative areas in

Virginia. The important thing is to put on a full custody case and not focus solely on the issue of sexual orientation.

You may want to utilize an expert witness who can talk about the fact that children raised in same-sex households fare quite well and are not "turned gay" by being raised by a gay parent. Dr. Charlotte Patterson at the University of Virginia has researched this issue extensively and has written a number of treatises on the issue. But, most importantly, you want to go through each and every one of the child custody factors and show how the court should rule in your favor under each factor, regardless of sexual orientation. For more information about sexual orientation and family law, look for my upcoming book, *Protect Your Love.*

**Homeschooling**

Many parents, throughout Virginia and throughout the country, choose to homeschool their children. Homeschooling is legal in every state, and in Virginia the requirements for compliance with the law are minimal. Homeschooling becomes an issue in custody and visitation cases when one parent wants the child to be homeschooled and the other does not.

When parents have joint legal custody, they are supposed to try to reach consensus on educational issues. When one parent has sole legal custody, that parent can make education decisions unilaterally. However, if the other parent feels that the custodial parent is making poor decisions for the child, she or he can petition the court for a change in legal custody, or even physical custody, upon a showing of a material change in circumstances since the last custody order.

If you are in a custody dispute and must defend your decision to homeschool your children, you will need to be able to show the court that your children are doing well, academically, socially, and developmentally, in the homeschool environment. You may wish to utilize an expert witness to talk about the benefits of homeschooling and/or about homeschooling and socialization. There are many homeschooling organizations available which may assist you in gathering information and identifying potential expert witnesses.

Academically: Standardized testing is a well accepted method of measuring your children's academic process. If your children succeeds on standardized tests, it should not be difficult to show that homeschooling is working, academically. If your method of homeschooling, or unschooling, is one in which standardized testing cannot adequately show how your children are learning, you may want to put together a portfolio or video displaying how you homeschool and what children are learning. You may wish to have an educational assessment performed by an educational psychologist. Whatever method you choose, you will need to be able to show children's academic progress in your homeschool.

Socially: Many opponents of homeschooling cite socialization as their reason to object to homeschooling. There have been many studies which show that homeschooled children are socialized equally well or better than their public and private school peers. Dr. Susan McDowell has written a book in which she has reviewed the research on homeschooling and socialization. *See* Dr. Susan A. McDowell, *But What About Socialization* (Philodeus Press, 2004). In order to address any concerns that the court may have about children's socialization in the homeschool environment, you will want to be able to show the court what activities, homeschool groups, field trips, etc. in which children are involved and which give them an opportunity to interact with peers and engage with different types of people. You may also want to show a written schedule of your children's weekly or monthly activities and make a video or photo album showing your children engaged in activities with other children.

Developmentally: The court will want to know that your child's developmental needs are being met in the homeschool environment. Depending on your child's age, this may mean that your child is getting exercise and fresh air, that your child has a daily routine, or that he can shower and dress himself, do household chores, etc.

You may want to prepare an exhibit showing your child's routine, chores around the house, and any other matters that you determine are currently important to your child's development.

## Abuse

Abuse is probably the most difficult child custody issue. Unfortunately, abusive relationships tend to cause the highest rate of custody and visitation litigation. If you have been a victim of domestic violence, or if you are a parent trying to protect your child from abuse, you must tread very carefully. Do not ever assume that you will get custody because the father was abusive to either you or your child. Most abuse is very difficult to prove, and you will likely be accused of trying to undermine your child's relationship with his father for reporting the abuse. If at all possible, consult with an attorney who has significant experience in family law and abuse issues before you do anything.

The following is a series of tips to assist protective mothers in navigating the world of the court system, addressing how to avoid the traps that your abusive former partner will set in order to try to make you look like the crazy or unstable person he wants others to believe you are.

Avoiding the traps that make you look like you are the unstable parent:

1. <u>Forget Fair:</u> That's right, forget fair. Swallow the pill early and wholly. None of what is happening in your life is fair, and the court will not even the score. Never assume that the judge is going to hear you tell your story and then stand up for you. You can be sure that your children's father (and his attorney) will tell a very different story to the judge, and the judge will not magically know which story is the truth. In the courtroom, it is not about truth, it is about evidence. Do not get caught up with each and every time something happens in your case that is not fair. Save your physical and emotional strength to focus on your strategy.

Sometimes unfair can benefit you in the long run. Most batterers are narcissistic. Given enough rope, they often hang themselves.

Making things right in the system is a different battle than protecting your children. Do not try to fight both battles at the same time - protect your children first. Protecting your children is more important than being right about anything. Even if you do not agree with the rules, sometimes you have to play by them in order to win. Suffer fools if you must, and chalk it up on the "puke meter."

2. <u>Be aware of the effects of Post-Traumatic Stress Disorder.</u>

Protective mothers often find themselves in the midst of custody litigation following their own escape from ongoing abuse and control at the hands of the abusive parent. Because of this, the protective mother is often suffering from post-traumatic stress disorder (PTSD) while she is dealing with attorneys, custody evaluators, and guardians *ad litem*, and when she is sitting in the courtroom. The very fact that she is suffering from post-traumatic stress disorder can play right into the theory of the universe that the abusive parent wishes to promote.

Because of PTSD, a protective mother is often worn thin and frazzled: physically, emotionally, and cognitively disorganized. She is at the end of her rope and can appear to others to be crazy, just as the batterer repeatedly says she is. Because the batterer is so persistent, the protective mother has often exhausted her usual allies, including her family and friends, and has often been through a few attorneys before her case is through. She has insufficient financial, emotional, and sometimes legal support and appears to others to have few "believers."

A batterer has often conditioned his victim to appear as if she is overreacting. The abuse, even post-divorce litigation abuse, can be so subtle and insidious that its messages and effects are seen and felt only by the victim. They are inherent in the relationship. When the victim tries to point out the abusive tactics to persons outside the relationship, she appears to be overreacting to very minor and/or reasonable action on the part of the abuser. When the abuser then states that the protective parent is hysterical and overreacts to everything, he is believed.

Because the protective parent has lost faith in a system which has failed to protect her child and has allowed the batterer to have ongoing opportunities to further abuse her through litigation, the protective parent often appears angry and frustrated at the court system. The people at the top af the very system which is the subject of her anger and frustration are now charged with evaluating the reasonableness of her anger.

In contrast to the post-traumatic protective parent, the batterer will always appear calm, friendly, and helpful. The batterer will always be in control of his words, his gestures, and his expressions.

3. <u>Watch out for land mines.</u> Your ex will set them and then point his finger at you when you stumble into them, accusing you of "Parental Alienation Syndrome," the creation of Dr. Richard Gardner, which has not been accepted by the American Psychological Association, is not based upon good science, but which rears its head over and over again in custody cases with abusers. An example of this is the "friendly parent trap." The abusive parent makes an unreasonable request designed to catch you being an uncooperative co-parent. If you currently have physical custody, the father will ask for visitation over some period in which he knows that you have something special planned with your child, or he will ask for something that you know is not best for your child, like bringing your child back from visitation at an unreasonably late hour on a school night. If he currently has physical custody, he will ask you to forfeit an important visit or create a situation where it becomes terribly inconvenient for you to exercise your visit. He anticipates that you will react in an angry and uncooperative manner which he will use as an example in court of how you create interparental friction. How you react to these set ups is extremely important and should be discussed with your attorney before you give any response, whatsoever, to the set up. If you are put on the spot and asked for an immediate response, your response should be, calmly, "I need some time to think about whether or not that idea is what is best for our child(ren)." Discuss with your attorney whether it is a point on

which you should give in (and show how exceedingly reasonable you are to his capricious demands), or whether you should counter with a calm, "No, I do not think it would be best for our son to go to poker night at Hooters with you this Wednesday night, but he would love to go bowling after school on Wednesday, if you would like to take him." When you decline the unreasonable request, always make a reasonable counter offer, and do it in writing. His traps depend upon your having a strong emotional reaction to his actions. If you react calmly, from a position of strength, the traps will fail. You may need an expert witness to testify about the fact that "Parental Alienation Syndrome" is bad science and is not accepted within the scientific community.

4. <u>Take back the power.</u> The traumatic bonding which occurs between hostages and their keepers also occurs between abusers and their intimate partners. The abuser creates a dependence on him and becomes larger than life and omnipotent in the eyes of his partner or former partner. He can elicit emotions from his partner at will - empathy, anger, guilt (even when the partner is the one who has been wronged), and feelings of powerlessness.

It is helpful to understand how the batterer operates. He uses coercion, power, and control. He has a sense of entitlement with, and ownership of, his partner/former partner and children. He uses manipulations, set ups, and mind games. The abuser projects what he is and what he does onto the subjects of his abuse, and he actually sees himself as the victim. He is a master of minimization of his own bad behaviors, denial, and blame shifting. He will use gaslighting, a technique of manipulating his victim and her surroundings so that she begins to think that maybe he is right, maybe she is crazy. The abuser will do anything to wear down his partner's self worth. He knows that he can elicit an emotionally charged reaction from her, and he depends upon this. You cannot, and the court cannot, change this pattern of manipulative behavior. Your awareness of it, coupled with your awareness of your own reactions to the behavior, can change the cycle. Remember, his scheme relies upon your reacting strongly and emotionally to his behavior.

5. <u>Do the unexpected.</u> Not responding the way an abuser anticipates takes away his power. If he pushes a hot button, respond with logic and emotional indifference. Go along with his ludicrous demand, or offer a reasonable alternative instead. He will become flustered. Practice being non-reactive. Rather than reacting, keep a fact log of the dates, times, and incidences of his immature and selfish behaviors. That way, rather than making you look crazy, his actions make him look unstable. He wants to keep you in a constant state of crisis. Remember, what is most immediate is often not the same as what is most important. Stay focused on your long term strategy. Every action does not require a response.

6. <u>Abuser's biggest weapons are also his Achilles' heel.</u> A batterer's inherent sense of entitlement and omnipotence can lead to carelessness. If he feels that he is above rules and court orders, give him some rope, rather than exhausting yourself in an effort to reign him in. He may just hang himself. Also, he is so accustomed to being able to manipulate your behavior that he will be lost if he is unable to.

His calm, cool and collected demeanor - if you think about it, that behavior is completely inconsistent with someone who is listening to evidence that his child is acting out, disclosing abuse, etc. If he were not the perpetrator, he would normally have *some* emotional reaction to hearing these things and would want to find out if the child is being abused by anybody. He would want there to be investigations, and he would be cooperating with authorities.

7. <u>Correct the context.</u> If your child's father has abused your child, once the abuse comes before the court, the abuser will file a petition for physical custody. He will then have turned the child abuse case into a child custody case. This changes all of the underlying assumptions, clouds the abuse disclosure in suspicion, dilutes the issue of abuse, and changes the focus and treatment. You need to clarify every step of the way that the abuse is not a custody issue. The disclosure of abuse preceded the abuser's campaign for custody.

8. <u>Educate the court.</u> Expert witness testimony on domestic vi-

olence and on child sexual abuse is extremely important, in some cases crucial. If the abuser presents evidence that he "passed" a psycho-sexual evaluation or a lie detector test, you may need an expert on rebuttal to explain why an incest perpetrator can "pass" such an evaluation and/or lie detector test. Make each witness' testimony fit together. Show that each of your actions was a reasonable reaction to the events as they took place. Show why your story makes more sense than his, why your reactions to disclosures of abuse make more sense than his reactions.

## Relocation

Relocation with children, either out of the state where the other parent is living, or a significant distance within the same state, is very difficult to do, particularly in Virginia. In Virginia, the parent proposing the move has to prove that the move is in the best interest of the child, independently of any benefit that the proposed move may confer on the custodial parent. A parent who is attempting to relocate with a child should thoroughly research the area of the proposed move. She should be able to show pictures of the home to which she wishes to move, the neighborhood, the school that the child would attend, and any church, daycare, or other place of importance to the child after the move. She should be able to show the quality of life and education available to the child after the move. If the child is engaged in sports or other activities, the parent proposing the move should research the resources for those sports or activities in the place where she wants to move. Perhaps most importantly, the parent wishing to move should have a visitation proposal for the non-custodial parent which offers enough time so that the move does not significantly interfere with the relationship between the non-custodial parent and the child. This will probably mean that most of the summer and holiday vacation time is spent with the non-custodial parent. The custodial parent should also have a proposal for how transportation will work for visitation. This proposal will minimize the impact of the move on the non-custodial parent's ability to spend time with the child. The parent should also be able to show how the child will be able to spend time with extended family members and other important people in the child's life after the move. It is crucial that the parent wanting to move can identify and prove that the move will somehow independently benefit the child.

## Special Needs Children

Custody and visitation determinations for special needs children can be very difficult, especially when the parents are not in agreement as to the severity of the child's needs and the proper course of treatment or other methods of addressing the child's special needs. It may be necessary to have your child's specialist in court to testify about your child's special needs. It may also be necessary to have your child's physical therapist, speech therapist, or occupational therapist and special education teacher, as well as any other professionals with whom your child works, present to testify about your child's needs and the scheduling concerns which may affect custody and visitation. It may also be necessary to bring in an expert on your child's condition to talk about recommendations and prognoses. Finally, you may want to make a "day in the life" video to show the day-to-day realities of parenting a child with your child's special needs and how well you and your child work together to meet those needs.

# 5 ALTERNATIVES TO LITIGATION

### Mediation

Mediation, under the right circumstances, can produce a resolution to your custody and visitation dispute. This resolution may be more closely tailored to the specific needs of your child and your family than anything a judge can come up with. Mediation is also far, far less expensive than litigation. Finally, mediation can resolve a dispute in such a way that it does not completely destroy any chance of friendship or alliance between you and your child's other parent. These relationships will almost certainly be destroyed by an ugly custody battle.

Mediation is probably not appropriate if there has been physical, verbal, or emotional abuse in the relationship, or if your child's other parent is extremely controlling, and you have any concern that you will not be able to stand up for yourself. In mediation, you do not have your own advocate. The mediator's job is not to make the outcome fair; it is to keep you focused on the issues and help facilitate communication so that you and the other parent can reach a resolution. The mediator is supposed to screen for cases wherein mediation would be inappropriate, but this process is not failsafe.

If you think that mediation is appropriate for your situation, by all means, give it a try. If it does not work, you can always litigate. You do not have to come out of mediation with an agreement if you choose to terminate mediation. I recommend choosing a psychologist who regularly works with children as a mediator for custody and visitation matters. You can then draw on the mediator's expertise in coming up with solutions for your child.

## Collaboration

Collaborative practice is a relatively new method of dispute resolution, and one that can serve parents and children well in the context of child custody. In collaborative practice, you and your child's father enter into an agreement with your team of professionals in which you commit to resolve your differences without taking one another to court or using threats to take one another to court. You agree that you are going to treat one another with respect and focus on your respective interests to come up with a resolution that best serves your particular family. The resolution is reached through a series of collaborative meetings with the professionals involved in the process. They take place in the office of one of the professionals, in an environment which is far less formal and far more comfortable than a court setting. There is no game-playing, trickery, or possibility of loopholes.

Your team of professionals includes your attorneys and, depending on the model of collaborative practice that your attorneys use, may also include a collaborative coach for each parent, a child specialist, and a financial specialist. The collaborative coach is a therapist who assists you through the collaborative process, both outside of the collaborative meetings, when emotionally charged issues arise, and during the collaborative meetings, when discussions become difficult for you, and you need a time-out or assistance communicating your thoughts and feelings. The child specialist is a child psychologist who may meet with your children, and who gives suggestions to help you reach a resolution geared to the particular developmental and emotional needs of your children. If you have financial issues that need to be addressed, you may use a financial specialist to review your finances and make suggestions.

If you are able to use the collaborative process, you will likely end up with a parenting resolution which uniquely fits the needs and interests of your family. You will almost certainly end up with a better co-parenting relationship with your child's other parent than you would if you litigated or even mediated your dispute.

# 6 COURT 101

## The Stepford Wife Makeover

Even though you shouldn't have to, and even while the world is falling down around you, looking like what the judge thinks a mother should look like will help you tremendously. This is the time to succumb to patriarchal ideals of motherhood. Change the world later. This makeover not only includes your wardrobe, but your mannerisms and the way that you communicate with the judge and other important people in your case.

The most superficial change that can affect the outcome of your case is your wardrobe. At this point in your life, you may have to borrow clothes from your friends or visit a high-end consignment shop, but your clothing and appearance in court is very important to your case. Even if money is not a problem, and your closet is full of designer business suits, you probably want to wear something a little more maternal than that. While a business suit may convey that you are a successful, contributing member of society, you want the judge picturing you at a PTA function or soccer game, not a board meeting.

A nice, tailored suit in something lighter and less lawyer-looking than black, navy, or pinstripe is always a good bet. A knee length skirt is more motherly than slacks. Yes, it is old fashioned, but remember, in some states, female attorney hopefuls are still not allowed to wear slacks while taking the bar exam. This is the climate in which you are functioning. A soft-colored blouse or sweater and low heels complete the soccer-mom-going-to-junior-league-luncheon look. If you have or can borrow a set of pearls (they can be fake a la Barbara Bush) and earrings, even better. Your hair should look neat, but not severe. Even though it sounds silly and has nothing to do with the merits of your case, the judge will be watching you throughout your case, and the way you look will form a large part of the judge's opinion of your credibility and ability to function as a mother.

Always be courteous and polite to everyone in the process. If someone needs to play bad cop, let that be your attorney. The clerk and the bailiff are as important as the judge. Judges often ask their clerks and bailiffs about the behavior of parties when the judge is not in the courtroom. Likewise, if you behave badly in front of the secretary or receptionist of an evaluator or guardian *ad litem*, you can be sure it will have an impact on what kind of person that evaluator or guardian thinks you are. I know one guardian *ad litem* who has a hidden camera in the reception area of her office in order to see how parents behave with their children in the waiting area when they think no one is looking.

The guardian *ad litem*, custody evaluator, and other professionals have immense power in your case. Do not argue with them, even if they are wrong. Put your best foot forward. If they do something wrong or make a mistake, tell your attorney and let your attorney handle it. Remember, you must always be the good cop, your attorney can be the bad cop.

It is important to remember that the opposing attorney is not always a bad person. You may certainly disagree with her or him, or correct her or him, but do not argue or make it a personal battle with the attorney. She or he may not be personally invested in the case. Also, she or he may have fallen for the batterer's story, in which the batterer is the victim. Remember, your ex is convincing. He managed to pull you in at one time.

## What to Expect

Trials follow a basic format. The attorney for the **moving party**, or the party who is asking the court to make a ruling, first gives an **opening argument**. The opening argument is a summary of what the party is asking for, and what the evidence is going to show to support the court ruling in that party's favor. The responding party will then give an opening argument, stating what that party is asking the court to do and setting forth what the evidence will show in support of that party's request. Next, the moving party puts on her **evidence** through witnesses and exhibits. The responding party then puts on his evidence though witnesses and exhibits. The moving party will then have the opportunity to put on any **rebuttal evidence** that the party may have, which answers or disproves the responding party's evidence. The responding party may then have an opportunity for **surrebuttal**, where he can put on evidence to respond to rebuttal evidence. Next, the attorney for the moving party will give a **closing argument**, tying together the evidence that has been presented by both sides into an argument to persuade the court to rule in her favor. The attorney for the responding party will then give a closing argument, arguing how the evidence that was presented supports the court's ruling in his favor. The moving party will then have a chance to briefly respond to the responding party's closing argument. Because the moving party has the **burden of proof**, meaning that it is her responsibility to prove to the court that the court should make a change from the status quo, she gets the last word. Either before or after closing arguments, the guardian *ad litem* will give an argument that includes her recommendations to the court, and what those recommendations are based upon. The judge may make a ruling at that time, or may tell the parties that she wants to further consider the evidence and make a ruling, either orally or in writing, on another date.

Sometimes the format gets thrown off track a bit. A trial may be continued because somebody is ill or may start late because the judge's earlier docket runs overtime. Do not be surprised if you and your witnesses are stuck sitting around and waiting at the courthouse. Witnesses, especially experts, may be called out of turn in an effort to accommodate their availability. Often, custody and visitation trials are not finished in one day, and you will need to find another date that the court and all attorneys have available to finish the trial. This date could be several months from the original date. Your attorney will be accustomed to these things happening, as they are normal occurrences for a trial lawyer. They may be stressful for you, but you should be prepared that these things do happen. If you start with the expectation that your trial may not start and end as planned, you are less likely to become frustrated if these things happen.

**Courtroom Etiquette**

If you are allowed to take your cell phone into the courthouse, make sure that it is turned off when you go into the court room.

When the judge enters the room, or any time she stands up, everyone stands up.

Do not speak unless you are asked a question. Refer to the judge as Your Honor.

Stand up when you speak to the judge.

**NEVER MAKE FACES IN COURT, I MEAN NEVER.** I cannot overemphasize this. You will hear ridiculous things in court. You will be made out to be a horrible person. Your ex will tell lies. His witnesses will tell lies. It doesn't matter. If your face is contorted and your eyes are rolling while these lies are being said about you, it will make the lies more convincing. If you keep a poker face while the lies are being told, the lies are far less credible. The judge sees you on the witness stand, but also watches your demeanor while the attorneys make their arguments, and the other witnesses testify. Many judges are convinced that they can see what is "really going on" in a case by watching the faces, gestures, and demeanor of the parties while the case is going on.

Likewise, if the opposing party or someone else is lying on the witness stand, do not say, "He's lying!" or begin gesticulating or scribbling notes to your attorney wildly. For one thing, if you and your attorney have prepared together sufficiently, your attorney will already know that the father is lying. Your attorney needs to be listening to what is being said on the witness stand in order to effectively cross-examine the witness. Furthermore, it makes you look like the crazy person that the witness has just finished saying that you are. If someone is lying, and you are not confident that your attorney is aware of the lie, calmly and quietly write a note and discreetly pass it to your attorney.

Remember, the judge does not have a crystal ball that reveals the truth to her or him. The outcome of your case does not depend on the truth, but on the evidence that is presented in court. Your presentation in court and your testimony are part of that evidence.

Always tell the truth, but don't spill your guts. While it may be cathartic to open up the floodgates and let it all come gushing out, litigation is not the appropriate forum for that catharsis. You need to speak in such a way that the evaluators, guardian *ad litem*, and judge are ready, willing, and able to hear you.

First and foremost, tell the truth. There may be some parts of your story that do not cover you in glory. You are human. We all have done a thing or two that we would rather not have to talk about in a custody battle. Besides the fact that lying under oath is wrong and illegal, it is far better to appear to be a credible person than a liar. The truth, with explanation, is always better than a lie or half-truth.

When you are testifying, organize your thoughts before speaking. If you need a moment to gather your thoughts before you begin, it is absolutely fine to take a moment to do so before you begin answering a question. When you are on the witness stand, make sure you are answering the question that is being asked. Do not lose the forest for the trees. Not every detail needs to be presented in court, and diluting the important points with superfluous details can detract from the evidence that will have the most profound impact on your outcome. Give facts and not conclusions. It is the province of the court to make conclusions. Your job is to present the facts in a way which leads the judge to reach the correct conclusion herself/himself. Finally, remember that the judge's attention may drift. Give the important details, but be focused and succinct.

When speaking with evaluators, guardians *ad litem*, and other potential witnesses, **do not assume** that you can trust people just because they are supposed to be helping you or your children. Talk to your attorney before speaking to anyone about your case. Do not attempt to publicize your case without first discussing it with your attorney. Remember that you are only guaranteed confidentiality when you are speaking to your attorney outside the presence of anyone except your attorney and her/his agents. You have no privilege of confidentiality with the guardian *ad litem*, your child's therapist, or an evaluator. Also, be aware of the possibility that you may be taped. In addition, there may be a tracking device on your vehicle, your house may be bugged, and there may be spy software on your computer. Paradoxically, it is important not to tell people other than your attorney if you think that you are being taped or spied upon, as it will make you sound paranoid.

## Surviving Cross-Examination

When you testify, your attorney will ask you a series of open-ended questions. This is called **direct examination**. Your attorney cannot ask you "yes" or "no" questions, or **leading questions**, on direct examination. She will have to ask you who, what, where, when, why, and "what, if any..." questions. In response to these questions, you will tell your story. You should work with your attorney ahead of time so that you will know what questions to expect and so that your thoughts are organized in your head. That way, you will be more likely to maintain the judge's attention by presenting only relevant information in a cohesive manner.

After you give your direct testimony, the opposing attorney has the right to **cross-examine** you. The attorney can ask you about any subject matter brought up in direct examination and can do so by asking leading questions. This is the opposing attorney's opportunity to try to trip you up and fluster you. The three most important things that you can do to survive cross-examination are: 1) listen carefully, 2) only answer what you are asked, and 3) do not lose your temper.

Listen carefully: When the opposing attorney asks you a question, and you answer the question, you are presumed to be answering the question that is being asked. Often, cross-examination questions begin with "Isn't it true that..." You absolutely must make sure to listen to the words that the attorney uses before agreeing or admitting to what you are being asked. It is okay to take a moment to think about what was asked before you answer.

Only answer what you are being asked. If your attorney asks you if you know what time it is, what will you tell her? If you give her the time, you are answering too much. She asked you if you knew what time it was. The answer should be yes or no. It is the opposing attorney's job to elicit testimony from you on cross-examination. Do not do her job for her. She will probably be asking you yes or no questions, and most of your answers should just be yes or no. Sometimes, it is appropriate to clarify your answer or clarify a variation between the way the question was asked and your answer, but you do not want to spill your guts when answering cross-examination questions. If your attorney objects to a question that is asked, do not answer until the judge has decided whether or not you need to answer the question. After cross-examination, your attorney will have an opportunity to ask you more questions to clarify your testimony on cross-examination. This is called **redirect**. If your attorney thinks that one or more of your answers on cross-examination needs clarification or further explaining, she will ask you about that answer on redirect.

Do not lose your temper: The opposing attorney will likely try to fluster you or make you lose your temper during cross-examination. She will likely use a harsh tone with you, speak loudly, and be rude. You may see red, and your instinct will tell you to fight back by being nasty and sarcastic in your answers. Resist the urge. Custody cases are won or lost by a parent's demeanor on the witness stand. While the rest of the case may be he said/she said, the judge feels that she is getting a firsthand view of the "real truth" by watching the parents' behaviors for herself. **It is absolutely necessary that you stay calm.** And if you do so, it makes the attorney who is attacking you look bad, and it may make the judge sympathetic for you.

After you are cross-examined by the opposing attorney, and before your attorney has the opportunity to ask you questions on redirect, the guardian *ad litem* (if you have one) will have an opportunity to ask you questions. After those questions, the judge may ask you a few questions, as well. Pay close attention to any questions that the judge asks you, as you can usually get a good idea of what the judge thinks is important in your case by the questions she asks. Try to answer the judge's questions as thoroughly and respectfully as possible.

# 7 WORKING WITH AN ATTORNEY AND OTHER PROFESSIONALS IN YOUR CASE

## Working With Your Attorney

A few words about your attorney: You absolutely must have an attorney who "gets it," who understands your situation and does not second guess the gravity of your case. Your attorney must comprehend what she/he is in for. Attorneys often hate difficult custody cases because they are always hard fought, they never seem to end, and the money almost always runs out before the case does. Even if your attorney has the biggest heart in the world, she/he has staff and overhead expenses to pay, not to mention that she/he is probably in business so that she/he can pay her/his own personal bills; and time working is time away from her/his own family. Make sure your attorney is up for the fight, and make sure your attorney is being paid. You have the right to expect your attorney to work and fight hard for you, and your attorney has the right to expect to be paid for her/his services. Also, you have to have someone in your corner other than your attorney. Having a friend, family member, or therapist to provide you emotional support is an absolute necessity. Your attorney will burn out too early if you rely on her/him as your main source of emotional support. Also, many really great attorneys are lousy at providing emotional support.

Teamwork. You should acknowledge that your case is more important to you than it is to your attorney. Even if your attorney has her heart and soul in your case, it is your life and your child. You and your attorney should be on the same page, even if that requires occasional meetings with your attorney just to check in and make sure you both agree and see the same things with the case. You should plan your communication in advance, or it may not happen as it should. Trial lawyers spend most of their time outside of the office, and it can be difficult to get them on the phone. Set a series of appointments with your attorney well before your trial date. If you are having a difficult time reaching your attorney by phone, call the office and schedule a telephone appointment. See if your question is one that can be answered by a paralegal. Also, faxes and e-mail can be more effective means of communication than telephone calls, but do not turn into the boy who cried wolf. If you fax your attorney daily, your faxes will not get the immediate attention that they receive if you only send them when there is an important, time sensitive issue. If you feel that your attorney may not be on the same page as you, get the kinks worked out well before trial day.

If you become dissatisfied with your attorney, do not fire him or her impulsively. Make a consultation with one or more reputable attorneys to get a second opinion. Often, there are minor kinks in communication that can be resolved in a short meeting. If so, stay with your attorney. It will be far more expensive to bring a new attorney up to speed, and your new attorney may not become as invested in your case as your original attorney. Also, many judges see it as a weakness in a party's personality or case if that person has switched attorneys. If, however, you have lost faith in your attorney, hire a new attorney in whom you do have faith. You need to trust that your attorney is doing her best for you, and you need to be able to work together as a team. If you cannot afford an attorney, read and re-read these tips until you have fully absorbed them, and do the best you can.

## The Guardian *Ad Litem*

Speak to your attorney before meeting with the guardian *ad litem* (or "GAL"). Remember that, unlike with your attorney, you have no privilege of confidentiality with the guardian *ad litem*. Anything that you say to him can be repeated to the other side. Anything that you give to him can be shown to the other side. You will have to use finesse in talking about your child's other parent. You will need to give the GAL pertinent information about his parenting skills and any concerns that you have, but DO NOT go into the meeting with the GAL bashing the other parent. If you do, you will be seen as someone who cannot co-parent or facilitate your child's relationship with her father. So while you do need to share any concerns you have about the other parent, you want to do it in a matter of fact way and not dwell on it. You should spend more of your time and energy focusing on the positives of your own parenting of your child. Remember that the GAL's recommendation to the judge holds a great deal of importance to most judges. This is an important person with power in your case. It is not worth getting into an argument with the GAL over minor details, whether or not you think he is doing a good job, or like or dislike his treatment of you. Address any concerns about these things with your attorney, and let your attorney handle it. Unfortunately, there is a bit of a popularity contest going on between you and the other parent for the GAL's recommendation. Although it should not be that way, you need to acknowledge it and govern yourself accordingly.

**Custody Evaluators and Other Forensic Evaluators**

Speak with your attorney before meeting with custody evaluators or other forensic evaluators. Much like with the guardian *ad litem*, you do not have confidentiality with evaluators. Also, you must use the same finesse that you used with the GAL to relay your concerns about the other parent without bashing him. Evaluators are very much on the lookout for a parent who seems vindictive or overly negative about the other parent. Finally, if you have concerns about the way the evaluator is doing his job, address them with your attorney, not directly with the evaluator.

# 8 10 TIPS FOR REPRESENTING YOURSELF IN COURT

1. Most of the work in a trial is done before you ever go to court. You must be proactive. Talk to everyone involved after being advised by your attorney. Evaluators, guardians *ad litem,* social workers and therapists will have mostly formed an opinion before the hearing. You must be involved in the formation of these opinions.

2. Your conduct in the pre-trial phase is crucial. You are living under a microscope at this point in your life. Assume everything you do or say is known or knowable to your child's other parent and his attorney.

3. Discovery is a tool that attorneys use to find out facts, along with the opposing party's theory of the case and trial strategy. Extensive discovery is absolutely necessary in difficult custody cases. Dig! Dig! Dig! The truth is out there. Do not forget cell phone records; they can be very helpful. Plot every fact that you find out on your timeline of events. Connect the dots. The extensive quantity of relevant facts in difficult custody cases must be organized and digested well before trial.

4. File appropriate pretrial motions. If the other side has disclosed in discovery that they intend to introduce evidence which may be inadmissible, pretrial motions can narrow the issues and exclude evidence which should not be allowed. Trials can be won or lost on pretrial motions.

5. Your courtroom demeanor is crucial. Judges often see ***pro se* litigants** (people who represent themselves in court) behaving outrageously. Of course you are more impassioned about your own

case than any attorney could be, but you must be organized, logical, and not overly emotional if you want to be taken seriously by the judge. At the same time, you want to be yourself and not appear to be trying to be Perry Mason.

Make sure there is a court reporter at your trial. If there is an attorney on the other side of the case, call his office and find out if he has hired a court reporter. If not, call one yourself and arrange to have the court reporter appear for your trial. You can look in the phone book for court reporters. It is important to have a court reporter for several reasons. First, if you want to appeal your case, you will have to have a record of the evidence that was presented in court. Second, as a *pro se* litigant, you may get bulldozed without a court reporter taking down everything that is said by the other attorney, the guardian *ad litem*, and the judge. Third, if someone lies on the witness stand, you will have proof. Finally, if you disagree over whether a proposed written order accurately reflects what the judge ruled, you can simply order the judge's ruling to be transcribed, and you will have it in black and white.

Put together your evidence before you go to court. You know the story that you want to tell. Find witnesses who have firsthand knowledge (they observed it themselves) of events, and determine what testimony you want to elicit from each witness. Also, determine what exhibits each witness can authenticate (the teacher can talk about notes that she sent home, the pediatrician can talk about medical records written by him, etc.). Put together a trial notebook that has an outline of your opening argument, your witnesses in the order that you plan to call them, the witnesses that you think the father will call, and your closing argument. Make a tab for each witness and put in the questions that you plan to ask the witness. For each exhibit that you plan to introduce, make three copies: one for the opposing party, one for the guardian ad litem, and one for yourself. You will give the original to the judge. Put your exhibits and copies under the tab for the witness that you plan to use to introduce the exhibit.

To introduce an exhibit, you will need to hand a copy to the guardian *ad litem* and the opposing attorney. You will then want to show the exhibit to the witness. You will need to ask the judge's permission to approach the witness before you walk up to the witness. You will then ask the witness to identify the document. You must then ask the judge for permission to approach the bench to hand the exhibit to the judge. The judge may instead have the bailiff take the exhibit to the judge. You will then ask the court to mark the exhibit (to avoid confusion in custody cases, I usually have exhibits marked and identified as "Mother's Exhibit #___." instead of Plaintiff's or Defendant's. You say that you move the exhibit into evidence. The opposing attorney may make an objection to the document's admission into evidence, particularly if the document has not been properly authenticated.

**What is Hearsay?** A document or testimony may be objected to if it is hearsay. Hearsay is an out-of-court statement which is being offered in court to prove the truth of the matter asserted (in the statement). For example, if your neighbor told you that she saw your child's father drive down the street with the child unbuckled and hanging out of the car window, you could not testify that your neighbor told you that. That would be hearsay because you would be offering an out of court statement (your neighbor's statement to you about what she saw) as proof of what she said in the statement (to prove that your child's father drove down the street with the child unbuckled and hanging out of the car window). That is hearsay and is inadmissible as evidence. Your neighbor could come in and testify as to what she saw, as she is the one with firsthand knowledge and can be cross-examined about what she saw, whether she's sure it was your child's father, etc. But you cannot testify about what she said she saw. Like testimony, documents can be hearsay, which is why it is necessary to have documents properly authenticated.

An out of court statement that is not being offered to prove the truth of the statement is not hearsay. For example, if your child came home from visitation with her father and said, "Mommy is nasty," it would not be hearsay for you to testify that she said that.

You are not trying to prove that you are nasty, you are simply trying to prove that your daughter said that when she returned from visitation. Because the statement ("Mommy is nasty") is not being offered to prove the truth of the matter stated (that Mommy is nasty), but is being offered for a different reason, it is not hearsay.

There are a number of exceptions to the hearsay rule, but an in depth discussion of the rules of evidence is outside the scope of this book. If you are representing yourself, it is worth your while to go to your local law library and find a book on evidence.

Once you have presented your evidence, through direct examination of your witnesses, presentation of exhibits, and cross-examination of the other side's witnesses, you will each give closing arguments. While you will need to adapt your closing argument to the evidence that was presented, it is helpful to have your closing argument prepared before you go to court. Many attorneys write their closing argument first, and then plan their witnesses and exhibits around the argument to make sure that all of the information in the closing argument has been properly presented as evidence before the court. Make sure that you behave in a professional manner throughout the trial. If the judge rules against you, save your reaction until you are out of the courthouse and in your car. Likewise, if the judge rules in your favor, do not gloat. Chances are, you will be in front of the same judge and court staff again, and you do not want to be remembered as a sore loser or a gleeful winner in the eyes of the judge, clerks, or bailiffs.

6. Put yourself in the judge's place. Your judge does not have any background into your situation except for the admissible evidence presented in court. The judge may not ever see your children and will never be as invested in them as you are. The judge is seeing you and your child's father for the first time, and he will only be able to make decisions based upon on what he sees and what evidence is presented.

7. Unravel the facts. The other parent may present a story that seems very simple and easy to swallow. The truth is often far more difficult. Concise and accurate presentation of facts is crucial.

Timelines, charts, graphs, videos, and other forms of demonstrative evidence which break down cumbersome amounts of information into tangible and easy-to-read exhibits can be better ways of producing evidence than lengthy testimony about facts that seem less important when taken individually. The truth is essential. If you did something that makes you appear less than perfect, explain why you did what you did. Remember, you are presenting facts, not opinions. Let the judge form the correct opinion himself, based upon your presentation of the evidence.

8. Weave the facts. Fit individual facts, which seem unimportant when taken separately, into the larger context. Make sure that you take all of your evidence and present it in such a way that the end result is a cohesive story that can be comprehended by someone who did not live it.

9. Poke holes in his story. Nothing can be as simple and black-and-white as his story will be. Find the holes. Dig, dig, dig in preparing the case. Find the truth, then find the admissible evidence.

10. Let your closing argument be the lightbulb over your judge's head. Highlight the very best evidence supporting why your version is the truth, and the father's cannot be.

# 9 THE SHORT LIST - THE 10 MOST IMPORTANT THINGS TO REMEMBER IN YOUR CUSTODY AND VISITATION CASE

1.  Bashing your child's other parent will get you nowhere. In fact, it may lose your case.
2.  Be prepared to address all of the child custody factors, showing why each factor supports your desired outcome.
3.  Live as if you have a private investigator following you at all times.
4.  Figure out how to tell your story through admissible evidence.
5.  Work as a team with your attorney. Assist in gathering and organizing information.
6.  Remember that guardians *ad litem* and court-appointed evaluators are relied upon heavily by judges. Prepare with your attorney before meeting with them.
7.  Always tell the truth, but don't spill your guts. Be ready to address and explain unflattering facts.
8.  Focus on the positive. Be able to show the court the unique and wonderful aspects of your parenting.
9.  Come to court prepared. The more prepared you are, the less nervous you will be.
10. Your courtroom demeanor may be the most important facet of your case. Do not make faces and do not lose your temper, no matter what.

# ABOUT THE AUTHOR

Kristen D. Hofheimer is a family law and civil rights attorney based in the Hampton Roads area of Virginia, focusing on the family law needs of women and the LGBT community. A partner at HOFHEIMER/FERREBEE, P.C. (virginiadivorceattorney.com) and THE FAMILY EQUALITY LAW CENTER (protectyourlove.com), she practices throughout the Commonwealth of Virginia and has written extensively on family law issues. Kristen has served as president of the Family Law Organization of Greater Hampton Roads, has served on the Virginia Beach Bar Association's Juvenile and Domestic Relations District Court's Bar/Bench Liaison Committee, the Virginia Trial Lawyer's Association's Family Law Legislative Committee, State Liaison for the American Inns of Court, and was named as one of Virginia's Rising Stars in the 2008 edition of Super Lawyers.

WA